INTERACTIVE WORKBOOK

Loving God with All Your Mind

Elizabeth George

HARVEST HOUSE PUBLISHERS
EUGENE, OREGON

About the Author

Elizabeth George is a bestselling author who has more than 7 million books in print and is a popular speaker at Christian women's events. Her passion is to teach the Bible in a way that changes women's lives.

For information about Elizabeth's speaking ministry or to purchase her books visit her website:

www.ElizabethGeorge.com

Elizabeth George
PO Box 2879
Belfair, WA 98528

LOVING GOD WITH ALL YOUR MIND INTERACTIVE WORKBOOK
Copyright © 2010 by Elizabeth George
Published by Harvest House Publishers
Eugene, Oregon 97402
www.harvesthousepublishers.com

ISBN 978-0-7369-3030-7 (pbk.)
ISBN 978-0-7369-3413-8 (eBook)

SFI Certified Sourcing
www.sfiprogram.org
SFI-00453

SFI label applies to text stock

Printed in the United States of America

16 17 18 / ML-NI / 10 9 8 7 6

Contents

Session 5: Living Out God's Plan—Jeremiah 29:11

Session 6: Accepting the Unacceptable—Romans 11:33

*I*ntroducing You to
Six Life-Changing Bible Verses

⸙

*I*magine two Christian women experiencing the exact same tragedy. It is sudden, unexpected, and traumatic. And it's so devastating that it may take weeks or months before life returns to normal.

Though they both face the same crisis, they respond in completely opposite ways. One falls apart from worry and discouragement. And the other, though somber, draws from an inner reservoir of strength and peace that can only come from a quiet yet firm confidence in God.

Same circumstances, but opposite reactions. What would account for the difference? As you'll soon see in this study, a Christian's reaction to adversity all comes down to placing a very real trust in God's commands and promises.

In the early years of my Christian life, I became depressed easily. But that changed dramatically when I realized the significance of what the apostle Paul wrote in Philippians 4:8. There, he commanded believers to think upon what is true and right instead of that which is speculative and wrong. I discovered that when I obeyed Philippians 4:8—and focused my mind on what was true and right—my negative thoughts would fade away.

Philippians 4:8 literally transformed my life. It's one of six verses that are very near and dear to my heart because it has helped me so much. And my prayer is that you'll have the same experience as you become more intimately acquainted with the six verses I share in this book. These passages are all precious promises from God—promises that will help you respond to life's crises with real and lasting peace, hope, and assurance.

I first shared these six life-changing passages more than a decade ago in my book *Loving God with All Your Mind*. This resource is now available for you to view on DVD, and this interactive workbook is designed to supplement the DVD sessions as well as provide new practical applications that will spur you toward greater spiritual growth.

In this workbook, you'll notice each DVD is broken down into four parts, or days. This will allow you to take time to carefully explore each promise in greater depth…and learn ways you can apply them so as to experience real change in your life.

Along the way you'll find yourself becoming more and more a woman who loves God with all her mind. May you be blessed as abundantly as I have by these six Bible passages!

In His love,

Elizabeth George

Thinking on the Truth

Finally, brethren,
whatever things are true,
whatever things are noble,
whatever things are just,
whatever things are pure,
whatever things are lovely,
whatever things are of good report,
if there is any virtue and
if there is anything praiseworthy—
meditate on these things.

PHILIPPIANS 4:8

℘ay 1—How Your Thoughts Affect You

ave you ever noticed how much your thoughts can affect the way you feel? You've probably had the experience of greeting a dear friend at church, only to get a curt response. Puzzled, you may have thought, *She must be angry with me.* Or, *What did I do to offend her?* And as you pondered your friend's reply, your mind may have imagined all sorts of negative possibilities. Though you didn't know why your friend reacted as she did, you began to assume something was wrong...with *you.*

When these kinds of negative thoughts take hold in your mind, they can easily lead you to feel discouraged, defeated, or angry. But what if your friend isn't upset with you at all? What if she was simply in a rush? Or her children had given her a hard time as she prepared them for church? Or she'd had a particularly difficult week at work?

That's just one example of how mere speculation in the mind can cause very real negative feelings. We imagine that we're the problem, when that's not the case at all! And we let our imaginations pull us down.

I confess I have been guilty of this. Whenever I dwelled on what I perceived as my failures and shortcomings, I would succumb to depression.

It was during one of my heavy moods that the apostle Paul's words in Philippians 4:8 caught my attention as never before: "Whatsoever things are true...think on these things."

Suddenly I realized my negative feelings were based on thoughts that weren't true or real. I had let my imagination second-guess God and the people around me.

I was encouraged—and excited!—about my discovery. I began to evaluate my daily thoughts in light of Philippians 4:8. And as the weeks went by, I realized just how many of my thoughts were based on imagined outcomes instead of truth. I learned Philippians 4:8 was God's solution for my struggles with worry and fear.

Truly, this is a life-changing verse. Together we're going to learn how to apply it. We'll find out how we can replace our anxieties with peace of mind, our fears with confidence, and our despair with hope.

Interacting with God's Word

"Whatsoever things are true...think on these things" is a command. It's not a suggestion or tip. And where can we find truth? In God's Word. Scripture provides for us the "curbs" that help keep our thoughts on the right path.

1. According to the following verses, in what ways does God's Word help us?

Psalm 119:11—

Psalm 119:105—

Psalm 119:165—

2 Timothy 3:16-17—

1 Peter 2:2—

2. How are you doing in terms of letting God's Word shape your thoughts? What are some ways you can improve in this area?

Stepping Toward New Growth

Paul said we are to think on whatever is true. What are some examples of untrue thoughts you've had?

What are the dangers of thinking untrue thoughts?

What are the benefits of focusing our thoughts on the things that are true and real?

When a thought first arises in your mind, what should you do?

Loving God with All Your Mind

Read Psalm 77:1-15, then answer the following questions:

How would you characterize the psalmist's thoughts and feelings (verses 1-4)?

What kinds of questions did the psalmist ask during his struggle (verses 5-10)?

What did the psalmist realize he needed to do (verses 11-12)?

How would you describe the "change in perspective" the psalmist expressed in verses 13-15?

At the beginning of Psalm 77, the psalmist was focused on his troubles. By the end, he had turned his attention to God. The psalmist went from gazing inward to looking upward. From doubting God to trusting Him. From feeling troubled to expressing praise.

So the next time negative thoughts arise in your mind and you get down on yourself, or you question God's love and care for you, check your focus. Are you looking down at your problem or up to God? Are you dwelling on things that aren't true or real? Are you letting the truths of Scripture act as curbs that restrain your thoughts?

*D*ay 2—Thinking True Thoughts About God

*W*hen life gets difficult, it's easy to let negative thoughts take hold in our minds. And the longer we grapple with life's problems or hard circumstances, the more we find ourselves saying things like, "God must not care about me, or He would have done something about this." Or, "I've cried out for help, and nothing is happening. Has God abandoned me?"

If you've ever had such thoughts, you're not alone. Through my years of ministry, I have had women pour out their hearts to me and wonder why God hasn't rescued them from their troubles. And many times they will conclude, "God must not love me."

I've also had times when I've felt that way. I'll experience a difficult trial, and I'll start thinking negative thoughts about God. When that happens, you and I need to stop and say, "Are these thoughts true about God? What does the Bible say?"

Whenever we find ourselves doubting God and fighting discouragement, we need to remember the apostle Paul's admonishment: "Whatsoever things are true...think on these things" (Philippians 4:8). Instead of entertaining wrong thoughts about God, we need to turn to the Scriptures and remember what is true and real about God.

Interacting with God's Word

1. What do the following verses say about the extent of God's love for you?

    Psalm 103:17—

    Romans 5:8—

    Ephesians 2:4—

    1 John 3:1—

2. Read Romans 8:35-39. What does this triumphant passage declare about the love of God?

    Based on the Bible verses above, what would you say is true about God's love?

3. What promises are you given in the verses below?

    Isaiah 41:10—

    Lamentations 3:25—

4. According to Psalm 27:14, how should you respond to life's difficulties?

Stepping Toward New Growth

When you pray about life's problems, God might not answer right away, but He *will* answer. That's why we're called to wait upon the Lord. If we try to resolve a problem in our own power, we will surely make matters worse. The better choice is to wait for God's perfect answer in His perfect timing.

What are some reasons God might not answer your pleas right away?

Read Proverbs 3:5-6, then answer the following questions.

With every matter in life, what are you commanded to do (verse 5)?

What are you commanded *not* to do (verse 5)?

To what extent are you to acknowledge God (verse 6)?

When you do so, what is the promised result (verse 6)?

I don't know about you, but I find great comfort in knowing that God has called me to simply *trust* Him. He doesn't tell us to figure out the *why* of our trials. All He asks us to do is trust Him.

What struggles can you turn over to God now? List them here, and take time to lift them up to your heavenly Father in prayer.

Loving God with All Your Mind

The next time you doubt God's love or care for you, ask yourself: Am I remembering what is true about God? Am I trusting what Scripture says about His love and care for me?

It is in God's promises that you will find peace, hope, and assurance no matter how difficult your circumstances. Though your problems might persist, you'll know the blessing that comes from resting in God's truths. You'll experience a fresh energy that enables you to hang tough and endure. And you'll move forward in God's strength and wisdom instead of relying upon your own.

$\mathcal{D}$ay 3—The Assurance of God's Forgiveness

When I first became a Christian, I went into the church's prayer room to share with a counselor about what had happened in my life and heart that week. I was given a packet of four memory verses that include promises or assurances the Bible gives to every believer.

One of those verses was 1 John 1:9, which says, "If we confess our sins, He is faithful and just to forgive us our sins and to cleanse us from all unrighteousness." As I studied that passage, I realized that when I sinned, I needed to confess it to God. So I began to include confession of sins in my prayers. And there were times when, after I agonized in prayer, I would think to myself, *But I don't feel forgiven.*

I've met other women who have struggled with that same thought. For some, it was because they couldn't believe God would forgive them. For others, it was because they had stumbled again and again into the same sin. That led them to assume that surely God had given up on them.

But when we say, "I don't feel forgiven," what have we just done? We've allowed our fickle human feelings to attempt to override the rock-solid promise from God that He would forgive us when we confess our sins.

Which should we trust more: our feelings or God's promises? What God says is true and real. So when our emotions stir up thoughts that are contrary to God's truth, we need to reject those thoughts. And instead, we need to rest in what God has said.

Interacting with God's Word

1. Read 1 John 1:9. What happens when you confess your sins?

   What two character qualities of God are mentioned in the verse?

   To what extent does God cleanse us?

2. Read Psalm 103:11-12. How does verse 11 describe God's mercy?

   What does verse 12 say God does with our sins?

3. According to Romans 8:1, what is your status in God's eyes?

Stepping Toward New Growth

Are there any areas in your life in which you feel unforgiven? Why?

What can you know with certainty from God's Word, based on 1 John 1:9, Psalm 103:11-12, and Romans 8:1?

If you're experiencing struggles in this area, spend some time in prayer right now with God. Ask Him to help you reject your wrong thoughts. And instead, place your full trust in God's promises alone. Ultimately, it's not a matter of how you *feel,* but what you *believe.* Do you believe God's assurance that you are forgiven? Why?

In what ways would your belief (and confidence!) in God's forgiveness help change your outlook on life?

Loving God with All Your Mind

Romans 8:1 begins with the wonderful proclamation, "There is now no condemnation to those who are in Christ Jesus." On the cross, Christ paid the penalty for your sin. There is no sin past, present, or future that can condemn you. You have been made right in Christ. God made Jesus, "who knew no sin to be sin for us, that we might become the righteousness of God in Him" (1 Corinthians 5:21).

Later in Romans 8, Paul goes on to ask, "Who shall bring a charge against God's elect?… Who is he who condemns?…Who shall separate us from the love of Christ?" (verses 33-35). The answer to all those questions? Nothing!

You are *forever* forgiven, and your salvation is *forever* secure. Isn't that a wonderful and liberating thought? Whenever you doubt that God has forgiven you, meditate upon these truths. Memorize them upon the tablet of your heart. Believe them without hesitation!

In light of God's forgiveness toward you, what are some ways you can show your gratitude to God?

$\mathcal{D}$ay 4—Taking Every Thought Captive

A vital part of real and lasting spiritual growth is taking our Bible knowledge and putting it into action. Merely *knowing* God's truth won't help us grow. If we really want to tap into the power of God's Word, we need to *live it out*.

So when it comes to the apostle Paul's command, "Whatsoever things are true...think on these things" (Philippians 4:8), how can we make that happen? How can we train ourselves to reject wrong thoughts and focus only on what is true and real?

Here is a three-step process that has helped me to change my way of thinking so I'm living in God's truth and bringing honor to Him:

1. Recognize the Command

   Jesus said, "If you love Me, keep My commandments" (John 14:15). Well, Philippians 4:8 is a command. It's not a suggestion. It's not optional. We're told to focus our thoughts on God's truth. Our thoughts are either right or wrong. That may seem a stern approach, but it's the only way to get rid of destructive and harmful thinking.

2. Respond in Obedience

   Second Corinthians 10:5 urges us to destroy "speculations and every lofty thing raised up against the knowledge of God," and to take "every thought captive to the obedience of Christ." That's *every* thought! Wrong thoughts that are left un-attended will lead us *away* from obedience to our Lord. Why? Because they're not true. Yield your every thought to Him!

3. Reap the Benefits

When we train our minds in this way, we will experience wonderful benefits, including...

- the joy that comes from pleasing God
- improved relationships with others
- less stress and more peace in everything we do
- spiritual growth and maturity

Interacting with God's Word

1. Are you taking your every thought captive to Christ? A good way to evaluate your thoughts is to measure them against Philippians 4:8. Read the verse, then answer the following questions:

What kinds of thoughts are we called to have?

By implication, then, what kinds of thoughts should we *not* have?

2. Now read Philippians 4:9. What does Paul ask his readers to do?

What benefit will Paul's readers enjoy as a result?

3. When it comes to training your mind according to Philippians 4:8, your sole guide is God's Word. Read 2 Timothy 3:16-17 and list all the specific ways the Bible can help you.

Stepping Toward New Growth

Can you think of a time when you failed to take a thought captive for Christ? What were the results?

How would the outcome have changed if you had yielded your mind to Christ?

Think of a recent time when you took a thought captive to Christ. What led you to submit that thought to the Lord?

How did you benefit from making the right choice?

If the outcome affected other people, how did it benefit them?

Is there anyone in your life you harbor negative thoughts toward? What should you do with those thoughts? How can you make that happen?

Loving God with All Your Mind

Scripture calls you to take *every* thought captive to Christ. Yet you've probably had times when you didn't want to. For example, maybe you wanted to nurse a grudge, or hurt someone who hurt you first.

But the command in 2 Corinthians 10:5 is clear. Only when you obey it will you reap the benefits. If you hold back even one thought, you are failing to love God with all your mind.

If you're thinking, *But that's hard to do!* you're right. Yet with the Holy Spirit's help, you are able. He will empower you. All you need is a willing heart. Take time now to pray and commit yourself to taking every thought captive to Christ!

SESSION 2

Winning over Worry

Do not worry about tomorrow,
for tomorrow will worry about
its own things. Sufficient for
the day is its own trouble.

MATTHEW 6:34

*D*ay 1—Overcoming Worry

⤜✵⤏

*W*orry affects all of us. And the potential sources of it are many—such as health problems. Financial hardship. Workplace stresses. The unknown future. Family difficulties. And unresolved sin, just to name a few.

Worries come in all shapes and sizes. Some have to do with minute, everyday routines. Others involve long-term decisions and events. And still others relate to circumstances that can affect us for the rest of our lives.

All too often, we worry about things that haven't even happened yet! We speculate, "What if…?" and we let our imagination wander. We envision worst-case scenarios that almost never happen. We waste a lot of thought, time, and energy dwelling on that which hasn't taken place and probably never will.

How can we break free from worry and enjoy lasting peace of mind?

Interacting with the Word

In Matthew 6:25-34, Jesus presents several truths that will help us win over worry. Remember how Philippians 4:8 urges us to *think* upon that which is true? Matthew 6 is filled with great truths we can believe in and *act upon*. These truths are the solution to anxiety…provided we listen to them.

What command does Jesus give in verse 25? Why?

What example of God's faithfulness does Jesus point to (verse 26)?

What ultimate point do you think Jesus is making in verse 27?

Why should we not worry, according to verse 32?

Rather than waste energy on worry, how should we occupy ourselves (verse 33), and what will happen when we do this?

What command does Jesus give in verse 34?

In summary, here are three important truths that will help replace your anxiety with peace:

> God is faithful and will take care of your essential needs.
> You will gain absolutely nothing from worrying.
> Do not worry about tomorrow. Focus on today alone.

Stepping Toward New Growth

Let's look a bit more closely at Matthew 6:34. Note Christ's formula for winning the battle over worry:

His command—

> *Do not worry about tomorrow,*

His insight—

> *Tomorrow will worry about its own things,* and

His challenge for you today—

> *Sufficient for the day is its own trouble.*

Our dear Lord knows how easily worry can overwhelm us—sometimes to the point of paralyzing us into inaction. So He tells us to stop looking ahead to the many responsibilities of tomorrow and instead, look only at the responsibilities of today. Today is all we need to cope with. Why? "Tomorrow will worry about its own things."

What worries are heaviest on your mind right now? As you write them down, place them in the appropriate column:

Worries About Today	**Worries About Tomorrow**

As you look at your lists, what observations come to mind in regard to your worries?

Are any of your worries too big for God to handle? If you resist letting go of your anxiety, what in essence are you telling God?

Loving God with All Your Mind

Worry seems to come so naturally, doesn't it? We probably don't realize how easily we slip into an anxious frame of mind!

That's why it's vital for us to memorize Scripture. When we've allowed God's truths to permeate into our minds and hearts, we're more likely to correct our course when we realize we've strayed from God's path for us.

Write the following verses below, then choose one to start memorizing right now. And let it help you take your thoughts captive so you can break free of worry!

Matthew 6:34—

Philippians 4:6-7—

*D*ay 2—Keeping Your Focus on Today

The tasks on our to-do lists seem to multiply all on their own, don't they? As soon as we wake up in the morning, we're already thinking about all the work that's ahead of us. And as we move through the day, more demands get added to our schedule. We then start feeling overwhelmed and wonder how we can possibly get everything done. Before we know it, instead of focusing on just one task at a time, we become stressed by the ever-growing list of things still undone. Rather than scaling the mountain of today, we gaze at the entire mountain range of tomorrows...and we find ourselves becoming paralyzed by worry.

Yet what did Jesus say? "Do not worry about tomorrow, for tomorrow will worry about its own things." Then He said, "Sufficient for the day is its own trouble" (Matthew 6:34). This powerful worry-buster appears in the Sermon on the Mount, and it applies to every child of God. Very simply put, Jesus commands us to not worry about tomorrow. Don't expend energy on that which isn't even here yet. Focus on today...and experience the peace of mind that comes from taking life one day at a time.

Over the next few lessons, we'll look together at a strategy for keeping our focus on today. We'll learn some practical guidelines that can help us obey Christ's command and win over worry.

Interacting with God's Word

1. Read Mark 1:35. How did Jesus begin His day?

   How would starting your day in this manner help you to avoid worry?

2. What does Philippians 4:6 tell us *not* to do?

   What are we to do instead, and how often?

   According to Philippians 4:7, what will we experience when we make our requests known to God?

   How are you doing in applying Philippians 4:6-7 to your life?

Stepping Toward New Growth

Guideline #1 for keeping your focus on today is to *prepare*.

Jesus began His day in prayer. It's when you're alone with God that you will receive everything you need for the rest of the day.

If you don't already, what time and place can you commit to cultivating this habit each day?

What are some of the responsibilities (and anxieties!) you can entrust to God right now?

Among the worries occupying your mind, which ones legitimately apply to today? Which should you set aside because they belong to tomorrow?

A good way to prepare for each day is to write a to-do list. What benefits can you see from taking this step before the day begins?

A quick tip: As you create your list, pay attention to prioritizing your tasks. While it may take a few extra minutes to do this, you'll be amazed at how much it helps your day go more smoothly.

Loving God with All Your Mind

God doesn't want you to worry. In fact, when you become anxious, you are saying, in essence, "God, I don't trust You with all that's happening. I'd rather have control over my circumstances than entrust them to You."

What's more, worry can hurt your health. It can affect also your relationships with other people. And ultimately it hurts your relationship with God because you're telling Him you trust your own wisdom more than you trust His.

When you catch yourself worrying...stop! Take time to pray. Consider how you can prepare for your day. Trust God to give you all that you need to endure. And don't look ahead to tomorrow.

$\mathcal{D}$ay 3—Scaling the Mountain of Today

When Jesus said, "Do not worry about tomorrow," He was teaching us to deal with the future in smaller, manageable pieces. He was urging us—literally!—to live one day at a time. This approach to life encourages us to break big projects into small tasks. And it reminds us to devote all of our spiritual, mental, and physical strength to where it's needed most—today.

When you keep your focus on today, you are much more productive. And at the end of the day, you will feel good about what has been accomplished, knowing that you made real progress.

With each new morning, you have the opportunity to apply Jesus' wisdom once again. You can get things done one step at a time. And before you know it, the mountains that once stood ahead of you will be behind you. Instead of experiencing anxiety, you'll know peace and satisfaction.

So what are the steps to making this happen? We looked at Guideline #1 (*prepare*) yesterday. Now let's consider Guidelines #2 (*plan*) and #3 (*proceed*).

Interacting with the Word

Guideline #2 has to do with *planning ahead*. When you look at your to-do list, prioritize the order of your tasks, and determine how to best accomplish each one, then you will approach your day with a sense of clarity and purpose. You'll know *what* needs to get done, *when* it needs to get done, and *how* it needs to get done. Now that's efficiency!

Read carefully through Proverbs 31:10-27. What kind of planning do you see evident in the tasks carried out by the Proverbs 31 woman?

Verse 13—

Verse 14—

Verse 15—

Verse 16—

Verse 18—

Verse 20—

Verse 21—

Verse 24—

Verse 27—

Without a doubt, careful planning was the key to this dear woman's productivity!

After you've made your plans, you're ready for Guideline #3—you're ready to *proceed* and put your plans into action!

Stepping Toward New Growth

What advantages can you see to planning your day?

When it comes to planning the routine tasks you do every single day, what changes can you make that will help you to do them more quickly, efficiently, or productively?

When it comes to the larger, long-term projects ahead of you (spring cleaning, painting a room, getting a child ready for college, making a career change, etc.), even though you need to look into the future to plan ahead, you still want to approach your task in today-sized portions.

What major project are you about to take on? What are some ways you can break it down into smaller, more manageable portions so that goals are more easily attained?

Even the best-planned days won't always go as expected. What appear to be interruptions may actually be God's way of saying, "Here's how I want to use you today." What attitudes should you cultivate for those times when God may move you from Plan A to Plan B?

After you've made your plans, you're ready to move on to Guideline #3, or *proceed*. If you're finding it hard to get started, what are some ways you can motivate yourself?

When it comes to stirring up the motivation to get things done, it's helpful to envision the end results. What are some blessings you or others have received from recent projects you finished? What blessings await you and others in the projects you've planned in the future?

Loving God with All Your Mind

Whenever you find yourself starting to worry, take a moment to assess your situation. Are you looking beyond today? If yes, then ask, What can I reasonably do today, and what should I hold off until later?

Then ask yourself, How can I break down today's assignments into smaller pieces? If even today looks too daunting, ask, What can I accomplish during this next hour? Or even during the next 15 minutes?

Set smaller goals, and reward yourself when you achieve them. Remember, your goal is for one good day. At the end of the day, you have a "pearl" you can add to the strand of your life. One of my favorite sayings is that "every day is a little life." Each good day becomes another pearl you can add to your strand…and before you know it, you'll have a lovely string of pearls! And remember God's promise to provide you with wisdom and strength! It all starts by bringing everything to Him in prayer.

$\mathcal{D}$ay 4—God's Promise to Provide Help

One of the biggest keys to winning over worry is trusting God to provide.

After you have poured out your heart in prayer and taken time to carefully plan your day, you're ready to proceed and climb the mountain of today. And as you step out in faith and obedience, you'll find that God provides everything you need to take on the responsibilities, problems, and even the interruptions that lie ahead.

God's faithfulness to provide for His children is evident again and again throughout Scripture. He protected and fed Hagar and her son in the desert when it appeared they might die (Genesis 21:14-19). He gave the Israelites food and water during their 40-year journey in the wilderness. He cared for the prophet Elijah in a time of great despair (1 Kings 19:1-8). When the young virgin Mary "was found with child of the Holy Spirit," God sent an angel to tell Joseph to take Mary as his wife and not divorce her—ensuring Mary would receive the protection and provision she needed (Matthew 1:18-25).

And the list goes on…all the way to God's promises to care specifically for you!

Interacting with God's Word

1. Read the following verses. What do they say about God's care and provision for you?

Psalm 33:20—

Psalm 56:8—

Psalm 115:11—

2. According to Philippians 4:19, what is the extent of God's provisions?

3. What invitation are you given in 1 Peter 5:7? (Be sure to note the word "all"!)

4. Read Philippians 4:11-12. What had Paul learned?

Now read verse 13. What assurance did Paul have, no matter how difficult or severe his circumstance?

Stepping Toward New Growth

As you proceed with your tasks for today, know that you are not alone! No matter what the challenge before you, God is ready to help you every step of the way. According to the following verses, what or how will He provide for you?

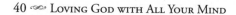

James 1:5—

Philippians 4:13—

2 Peter 1:3—

Are there any concerns on your heart that you haven't brought to God yet?

Share about a time when you experienced God's provision as you stepped out in faith. How did God provide, and what were the results?

Loving God with All Your Mind

God's promise to provide is an important assurance to remember. It will give you confidence when you need it most. It will help you at the times when you feel like giving up. As 1 Kings 8:56 says, "Blessed be the LORD...there has not failed one word of all His good promise." God is faithful. You can always count on Him. His promises never fail.

Write out Philippians 4:19 below, and if you haven't already, commit yourself to memorizing it. And whenever you begin to worry or become stressed, let your heavenly Father's promise of provision bring rest to your heart and give you peace of mind.

Pressing for the Prize

Brethren, I do not count myself
to have apprehended; but one thing I do,
forgetting those things which are behind and
reaching for those things which are ahead,
I press toward the goal for the prize
of the upward call of God in Christ Jesus.

PHILIPPIANS 3:13-14

$\mathcal{D}$ay 1—Remembering to Forget

$\mathcal{I}$n the course of our daily living, it's amazing how often something will prompt us to think about the past. For example, looking at a photograph, a school yearbook, a childhood possession will do that. Birthdays and anniversaries often cause us to recall people and events from the past. Even an act as simple as cleaning out your closet—and seeing long-forgotten items—may trigger thoughts of days long gone!

The woman you are today was largely shaped by your past. As you've progressed through life, you've learned lessons about God, the world around you, and yourself. And as you continue onward, it's important to know what Scripture says about how you view your past. If you're not careful, your past can interfere with what you do today. That's why the apostle Paul wrote some words of caution and exhortation in Philippians 3:13-14—another life-changing Bible passage that means a lot to me. And my hope is you'll find this passage a powerful help to you as well.

As Paul approaches Philippians 3:13-14 he urges us to grow spiritually mature by imitating Christ's example. Then when he writes this key passage, he lists three actions that help keep us moving forward in the Christian life:

> *Forgetting* those things which are behind and
> *reaching* forward to those things which are ahead, I
> *press* toward the goal for the prize of the upward call of God in Jesus Christ.

Interacting with God's Word

1. In Philippians 3:4-6, Paul mentions some of his past advantages and achievements. List them here.

   According to verses 7-8, how did Paul view these things from the past?

   What did Paul now desire?

   Verse 8—

   Verse 9—

   Verse 10—

2. Paul's view of what he counted as loss and gain is affirmed elsewhere in Scripture. Describe his perspective as stated in the following passages:

   Galatians 6:14—

   Philippians 3:20—

Colossians 3:1-2—

3. Read Matthew 6:19-20. What perspective does Jesus command us to have?

What key point does Jesus then make in verse 22?

Stepping Toward New Growth

There are two aspects to forgetting the past:

1. Refuse to rest on past accomplishments
2. Refuse to let past mistakes keep you from moving forward

For now we'll focus on the first aspect.

What are some of your past accomplishments—whether related to school, the workplace, or church?

How might your past successes hurt your future progress?

With Matthew 6:19-21 in mind, are there some earthly treasures (or distractions) that are robbing you of the time and energy you have for spiritual treasures?

What two or three ways could you make a more deliberate effort to build up your treasures in heaven?

Loving God with All Your Mind

A powerful way to truly love God with all your mind is to cultivate the habit of being more heavenly minded. That is, devoting more and more of your thoughts to the things of God.

In Colossians 3:16, Paul commands us to "let the word of Christ dwell in you richly." What are the different ways you can make that happen in your own life?

What specific steps can you take from today onward to apply Colossians 3:16?

As you focus your thoughts more on God and His Word, you'll find yourself thinking less about the past and earthly things!

$\mathcal{D}$ay 2—Forgetting the Negative Past

$\mathcal{I}$t's remarkable how the sins and mistakes of the past can rob us of joy, peace, and productivity. Though they are long gone and we cannot go back in time and change what happened, we let them pull us downward into discouragement and heartache. We let them hinder our spiritual growth or affect our relationships with family and friends. We even let them affect our relationship with God. For example, we might assume that our past failures somehow lessen the love God has for us.

For these reasons and more, Scripture pointedly commands us to forget the past and move on. When the apostle Paul wrote about "forgetting those things which are behind" (Philippians 3:13), he used forceful vocabulary. One Bible commentator wrote, "When Paul says that he forgets what lies behind, he refers to a type of forgetting which is no mere, passive oblivion. It is active obliteration, so that when any thought of…the past would occur to Paul, he immediately banished it from his mind…It is a constant, deliberate discarding of any thought of [the] past."*

So forgetting the past involves a deliberate, ongoing, and active rejection of thoughts about the past. It means saying, "I will not think about that."

---

* William Hendriksen, *New Testament Commentary—Exposition of Philippians* (Grand Rapids: Baker, 1975), p. 173.

Interacting with the Word

1. What counsel does King Solomon give in Proverbs 4:25-27?

   Verse 25—

   Verse 26—

   Verse 27—

2. In Proverbs 4:26, Solomon mentions "the path of your feet." According to Psalm 119:105, what helps us to stay on the straight path?

3. Both the Psalms and Proverbs speak of looking straight ahead, of staying on the right path. What are the possible dangers of...

   ...looking backward?

   ...straying off the path (hint: see Proverbs 4:27)?

   ...failing to consult the light of God's Word?

Stepping Toward New Growth

Have you recently spent time dwelling on certain negative thoughts? What impact are those thoughts having on your thinking, emotions, or actions?

What can you do to prevent those thoughts from affecting you?

One key way to deal with negative thoughts about the past is to replace them with positive thoughts about the present. What are some positive things you can think about? List them here.

If you struggle frequently with negative thoughts, you may want to write your list of positive thoughts on an index card and put it in a place where you will see it frequently. The card can serve as a reminder for you to change your thought patterns.

Loving God with All Your Mind

By now I'm sure you'll agree it doesn't make sense to dwell on the past. You cannot go back and change what happened. So it's much better to focus on the present and make the most of it. In doing so, you will free up your spiritual, mental, emotional, and physical energy. You'll enjoy today much more.

I don't remember where I heard it, but there's a saying I've memorized that has been very helpful:

> *Learn* from the past,
> *log* lessons from the past, but
> *leave* the past!

No less than the apostle Paul himself is our example. He knew the wisdom of "forgetting those things which are behind." Is there anything from your past you need to surrender to the Lord right now? Is there something that weighs heavily on your heart that you need to lift up to Him?

Take time now to do that. Stop looking back, entrust the past to God, and move on toward spiritual growth and Christlikeness!

$\mathscr{D}$ay 3—Pressing Onward

$\mathscr{I}$n the DVD session you just watched, I shared about a missionary who labored hard to teach some tribal people the meaning of Philippians 3:13-14: "Brethren, I do not count myself to have apprehended; but one thing I do, forgetting those things which are behind and reaching forward to those things which are ahead, I press toward the goal for the prize of the upward call of God in Christ Jesus."

Several days later, one of the missionary's students shared a poem he had written in response to the lesson:

> Go on, go on, go on, go on,
> Go on, go on, go on.
>
> Go on, go on, go on, go on,
> Go on, go on, go on.

And there were seven more stanzas exactly the same as those!

In many areas of life, repetition can be excessive or tiring. But in the Christian life, the repetition that leads to spiritual growth is a good thing. As we are "reaching forward to those things which are ahead," there are obstacles in our path that can trip us up or slow us down. We face all kinds of challenges and trials. And to overcome those, we need the kind of driven focus Paul calls for in Philippians 3:13-14—a focus that is repetitious in the sense that we keep on keeping on. How can we cultivate such focus?

Interacting with the Word

1. Read the following passages, and write what you learn about having a God-centered focus:

   John 6:38—

   John 17:4—

   2 Thessalonians 2:15—

   1 Timothy 6:11-12—

   2 Timothy 4:7-8—

2. According to Ephesians 5:15-17, why is a God-centered focus so essential?

3. With what frame of mind should we approach everything in life, according to 1 Corinthians 10:31?

4. Read 1 Corinthians 6:19-20. Why is it appropriate for us to live with a constant God-focus?

Stepping Toward New Growth

There is great value in determining your focus. When your goals are God's goals, you won't wander aimlessly through life and waste time and energy on fruitless pursuits. When you know exactly what to do, you'll make better choices and enjoy greater productivity.

Look back on your choices over the past week. What do they reveal about your focus?

Describe, in two or three sentences, the kind of focus you'd like to have.

What can you do on a regular basis to train or "work out" your focus?

The right kind of sleep, nutrition, and exercise can all have a positive effect on your focus. What changes can you make in these three areas to help you achieve better results?

Loving God with All Your Mind

When the apostle Paul speaks of "reaching forward" in Philippians 3:13, he is describing himself as leaning toward the finish line, eyes fixed on the goal. He is devoting all his energy—mental, emotional, and physical—to running the straight path God has set before him. He does not step to the side or slow down. He is driven, motivated, and focused!

In the space below, write a prayer to God and share with Him your heart's desire to stay focused. And from here onward, do whatever it takes to reach forward...and press on "for the prize of the upward call of God in Christ Jesus"!

$\mathcal{D}$ay 4—Running the Race Well

$\mathcal{P}$ersistence is a virtue well worth cultivating. It's when we hang in there and keep going—no matter how tough our circumstances—that we build strength and endurance. It's only through "staying the course" that we grow spiritually mature. When we give up, growth stops. But when we press onward we blossom, and God is able to use us all the more to His glory.

The difference between enduring and quitting can be huge. Imagine what would have happened if Moses had given up leading the people of Israel to the Promised Land. Or Esther had refused to take a stand when Haman wanted all the Jewish people killed. Or Daniel had bowed to Nebuchadnezzar's golden statue. Or the disciples had gone back to fishing instead of spreading the gospel message far and wide.

Persistence requires that we have the resolve to keep moving on. Paul wrote, "I *press* toward the goal for the prize of the upward call of God in Christ Jesus." He kept his eyes on the finish line. He wanted to run the race well. It wasn't easy. He poured all his energy into pressing on.

And was it worthwhile? Oh, yes! And the same will be true for you. You'll know great joy and satisfaction as you keep on keeping on.

Interacting with God's Word

1. When Scripture teaches the importance of pressing on, often we're given the illustration of running a race. For example, read 1 Corinthians 9:24-27.

   In what manner are you to run (verse 24)?

   What award are you running for (verse 25)?

   What did Paul do to his body, and why (verse 27)?

   What did Paul fear would happen if he didn't discipline himself (verse 27)?

2. Another "running the race" Bible passage is Hebrews 12:1-2. What are you told to lay aside, and why?

   How are you to run?

   Now read verse 2. Who is your example, and how is He described?

What did Christ endure, and what attitude did He have while He "kept on keeping on"?

3. Write, in your own words, what 1 Corinthians 9:24-27 and Hebrews 12:1-2 are calling you to do.

Stepping Toward Greater Growth

What weights or sins have you struggled with most recently that are slowing you down in the race?

What actions should you take to set aside those weights or sins?

It's important for you to realize that your day-to-day responsibilities—as a wife, mother, daughter, church member, worker, or student—have been entrusted to you by God and don't fall in the category of weights that hinder you. Scripture calls every believer to fulfill their obligations in a way that honors God. Rather, it's the daily choices you make about your time, your attitudes, your thoughts, and your actions that affect your ability to run well. As Paul said in 1 Corinthians 9:24-27, finishing well has everything to do with personal discipline.

Look at the list below. What choices can you make now so that you will run a better race during this next week?

My time—

My attitudes—

My thoughts—

My actions—

My finances—

Loving God with All Your Mind

The great nineteenth-century preacher C.H. Spurgeon said this about pressing onward. As you read, underline or mark any words or thoughts that especially speak to your heart.

> Keep not back part of the price. Make a full surrender of every motion of thy heart; labour to have but one object, one aim. And for this purpose give God the keeping of thine heart. Cry out for more of the divine influences of the Holy Spirit, that so when thy soul is preserved and protected by Him, it may be directed into one channel, and one only, that thy life may run deep and pure, and clear and peaceful; its only banks being God's will, its only channel the love of Christ and a desire to please Him.*

That is the kind of commitment that will help you to grow into a woman who loves God with all your mind. Won't you take time now to pray and ask the Lord to help you to run the race well?

---

* C.H. Spurgeon, *Spurgeon's Gems* (London: Passmore & Alabaster, 1859), pp. 14-15.

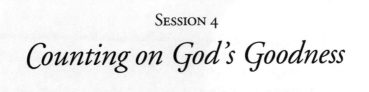

SESSION 4

Counting on God's Goodness

We know that all things
work together for good
to those who love God,
to those who are called
according to His purpose.

ROMANS 8:28

$\mathcal{D}$ay 1—Trusting the Lord and His Word

When things go wrong in our lives, it's easy for us to question God. When a dear family member or friend is grievously hurt or dies unexpectedly, when a horrific tragedy strikes, when life's trials push us to the breaking point with no solutions in sight, we're often tempted to doubt God. We struggle and ask, "God, how can You permit *that* to happen?" Or we exclaim, "God, this doesn't make sense!" And because we're unable to make sense of a terrible situation, we question God.

Yet when it comes to how we view the events of life, which are we going to trust: our thoughts and feelings, or the truths stated in God's Word?

There is an incredible promise in Romans 8:28 that offers great comfort for the hard times in life. There, Paul wrote that *all* things "work together for good" in the life of a Christian. At times we may find that hard to believe, but it's true. God has proven Himself faithful. We have to decide whether we'll trust Him.

Interacting with God's Word

When it comes to trusting God and His Word, I've found it helpful to learn as much as I can about Him. I use a gold marker pen to highlight all the attributes of God and the ways He works in His children's lives. The more I know about God's power, wisdom, love, compassion, and strength, the more I realize that when bad things happen, I need to simply rest and trust in Him.

1. What certainties can you trust about God, according to the following passages?

Psalm 34:19—

Psalm 72:12—

Isaiah 41:10—

Jeremiah 33:3—

Hebrews 13:5—

2. What certainties can you trust about the tough times in life?

Joshua 1:9—

Psalm 119:71—

2 Corinthians 12:9—

1 Peter 1:6-7—

James 1:2-3—

Stepping Toward New Growth

In those times when we doubt God's sovereignty or love, we need to remember that our feelings are unstable and uninformed. By contrast, God keeps His every promise. He has proven Himself again and again. He is worthy of our complete trust.

What are some examples of faulty thoughts we might have about God when we suffer?

What are two or three ways God has proven Himself to you in the past?

What benefits or blessings have you experienced as a result of persevering through a trial?

Which would you rather be: a Christian in God's care who faces frequent trials, or a non-Christian outside of God's care whose life is relatively free of difficulties? Why?

Loving God with All Your Mind

In 2 Corinthians 5:7, the apostle Paul wrote that we "walk by faith, not by sight." We're called to trust our heavenly Father, not our earthly senses. Faith will always endeavor to see the big picture behind life's difficulties. It will realize that God is present with us in all His wisdom, majesty, and strength.

Below, write about a situation that was difficult for you. First, describe it from your human perspective (your thoughts, how you felt, or how you perceived the circumstance).

Now describe it, as best you can, from what might be God's perspective. What might He have wanted to teach you?

When you trust that God really is in control and that He has your best in mind, you will have confidence and hope. You will know that even when you don't understand what's happening, He is watching over you and will work out all things for your ultimate good.

*D*ay 2—The Certainty of God's Promise

*W*e all know the pain that comes with broken promises. When someone fails you, usually you're left feeling frustrated and disappointed. And often you will find it hard to trust that person again.

By contrast, there's a tremendous sense of security that comes from someone who is good about keeping promises. She is true to her word and can be trusted. Whatever she says, she will do. So instead of anxiety and uncertainty, you feel peace and confidence.

When it comes to God's promises, you can have supreme security! He will never fail you. Sometimes decades or even centuries will go by before He fulfills a promise—but fulfill it He will.

Scripture is filled with promises that God will keep—no matter how bad things get. And Romans 8:28 is especially rich with promises that can give you comfort when life gets rough. Let's take a look at a couple key words within this promise that can give you bright hope even on the darkest of days!

Interacting with God's Word

In Romans 8:28, Paul wrote, "We know that all things work together for good to those who love God."

Notice the word "know." Paul didn't say, "We *hope* all things work together for good," or "We *think* all things work together for good." He said, "We *know*"!

1. On a scale of 1 to 10, how much certainty can you have with regard to the promise in Romans 8:28?

2. By contrast, how much can you trust your feelings or assumptions in response to life's trials? Why or why not?

3. Next, notice the word "all" in Romans 8:28. Paul didn't say, "We know that *some* things work together for good." He said "*all* things"!

   What are some of the worst imaginable disasters you could ever experience? How many of them can Romans 8:28 apply to?

   What does the certainty offered by the words "know" and "all" do to your perspective of God and His work in your life?

4. What do the following passages tell you about God's sovereignty?

Isaiah 45:6-7—

Job 38:4-7—

Psalm 135:6—

Stepping Toward New Growth

It's important to note what Romans 8:28 does *not* promise. It doesn't say your life will be free of problems. Nor does it say bad things in and of themselves will become good.

What it *does* say is that ultimately, God will somehow work out everything in your life—even the worst trials and circumstances—so that the end result is good.

With that perspective in mind, read Proverbs 3:5-6. What are you called to do? What does God promise to do?

Next, read 2 Corinthians 12:7-10. What two things did God tell Paul in verse 9?

What was Paul's response (verse 10)?

If you truly believed what is promised in Romans 8:28, what effect would that belief have on your attitudes and actions?

Loving God with All Your Mind

If you were to make a promise to someone and that person doubted that you'd keep it, how would you feel?

How do we malign God's character when we doubt His promises?

The remedy to unstable feelings or thoughts about God is to put your complete trust in what Scripture says is true about Him. And the more you read your Bible, the better you will get to know God (and love Him!). With that in mind, you may want to start saving a list of verses that affirm God's power, wisdom, strength, love, mercy, and so on. Or, mark those verses with a highlighter pen so you can find them more easily in your Bible. Then you can turn to those passages in your times of need.

A good place to start is Job 42:2. What encouraging truth does this verse offer to you? Write it below, and commit yourself to memorizing—and using—it this week.

Day 3—Trusting God's Good Purpose

All through the Bible, we find story after story in which God's people endure great pain or suffering. Yet in the end, God forges their negative experiences into positive results. Time and again, we see God redeem His children from seemingly hopeless circumstances and bring good into their lives.

Abraham was childless for decades, then became the father of a great nation. Joseph was sold into slavery and later thrown into prison, but went on to become a powerful ruler in Egypt. This put him in a position to save the Jewish people when famine struck the Middle East. After Moses wrongly killed an Egyptian he had to flee into exile for 40 years. God later brought him back to Egypt to free the Israelites and lead them to the Promised Land. Esther, by God's providence, became queen of Persia, making it possible for her to foil a plot that would have annihilated all the Jews. Daniel was preserved in the lions' den. And on and on it goes!

In every one of those situations, God took what was bad and turned it into good. And He still carries on that work today in your life!

Keep in mind that when Abraham, Joseph, Moses, Esther, Daniel, and others were in the midst of their difficulties, things looked dark and hopeless. They had no way of knowing whether their circumstances would take a turn for the better. And yet they persevered.

They didn't give up. They trusted God's good purpose. And they let Him do His perfecting work in their lives.

Interacting with God's Word

Usually when we're hurting or suffering, we're eager to escape our predicament. We want out. We want the pain to end. Yet life's trials have a way of forcing us to have greater faith in God. And as we're stretched to the limit, we learn new skills that make us more useful for the Lord's work.

1. According to 1 Peter 5:10, what are at least three or four results God can bring about from our suffering?

2. Read 1 Peter 1:6-7. What does Peter say trials do to our faith?

   What end result can come from our trials (verse 7)?

3. According to James 1:2-4, what does the testing of our faith produce?

4. Why can we "glory in [our] tribulations" (Romans 5:3-4)?

5. In Romans 8:18, what perspective does Paul say we should have in regard to our present-day suffering?

Loving God with All Your Mind

Think back upon the more recent trials you've experienced. Try to list as many of the blessings you and others gained from those trials.

As you look over your list, what specific thanks do you have for the work God has done in and through you?

After you have written your thoughts, spend some time in appreciative worship. Magnify the Lord for the ways He has worked out His good purpose in your life.

When He has tested me, I shall come forth as gold.
Job 23:10

$\mathcal{D}$ay 4—Navigating the Maze of Life

$\mathcal{W}$e all have people in our lives who are a blessing to us. And then we have people who make life a challenge! From our human perspective, we're surrounded by the good and the bad—some who lift us up, and some who pull us down. But from God's perspective, every person in our life has a purpose.

Though we may wish certain people weren't in our lives, Romans 8:28 reminds us that *"all* things work together for good to those who love God." If there's a difficult person in our life, it's because God has chosen to place that person there. He wants to use the people around us so that we might become more "conformed to the image of His Son" (Romans 8:29).

I have a saying that helps me a lot when it comes to relationships with people: "It's not them; it's Him." In other words, rather than blame those who make life hard for you, look up to God and know that He brought these people into your life. He has done this to stretch you, change you, strengthen you, and polish you.

Interacting with God's Word

1. What was Joseph's response after all the suffering he had endured because of the evil his brothers had done to him (Genesis 50:20)?

2. After Job suffered great calamity and lost everything he had, he said, "The LORD gave and the LORD has taken away" (Job 1:21). In saying this, he acknowledged God's sovereignty over the affairs of men. What did Job *not* do in response to his affliction (verse 22)?

3. Second Corinthians 12:7-8 tells us about a "thorn in the flesh" that tormented the apostle Paul. He prayed three times for God to remove it. What did God tell Paul, and how did Paul respond (verse 9)?

What conclusion did Paul reach about his affliction in verse 10?

Stepping Toward New Growth

As you can see from the above passages, when it comes to life's trials, perspective is everything. You have a choice: Will you let life's problems push you away from God? Or closer to Him? Will you complain about the inconveniences you're facing? Or will you praise God for the blessings that will eventually come forth?

Describe here, in your own words, the perspective you want to have when adversity comes your way.

Loving God with All Your Mind

Make a list below of the key people in your life—at home, at church, in the workplace, at school, and so on. Include those who are a blessing and those who are, figuratively speaking, a thorn in the flesh. In what ways do you see God using each person to help shape you?

Commit now to praying for those who make life hard for you. It'll help you to see those people through God's eyes instead of your own.

SESSION 5

Living Out God's Plan

For I know the thoughts I think
toward you, says the LORD,
thoughts of peace and not of evil,
to give you a future and a hope.

JEREMIAH 29:11

$\mathcal{D}$ay 1—Enduring Hardship

$\mathcal{W}$hen things don't go right for us, usually we assume that we're the victim of circumstances beyond our control. We view ourselves as victims, and blame other people or things for the mess we're in.

Yet Scripture clearly states God is sovereign over all the universe. Everything that happens has a part in God's plan. When the Israelites were taken into captivity by Babylon, they were baffled. Why had God allowed an unrighteous nation to conquer His own people? Why hadn't He protected them? Was He somehow weak and unable to prevent this injustice?

But God was still in control. He had a plan for Israel. He said, "I know the thoughts that I think toward you…thoughts of peace and not of evil, to give you a future and a hope" (Jeremiah 29:11). In the midst of their circumstance, the Israelites couldn't see what God was doing. God assured them with the promise of "a future and a hope."

When bad things happen to us, we need to realize God is still in control. Though we cannot understand His ways, He has a plan for us. In the long run, everything is going to be all right.

As we look to Scripture for guidance on enduring difficult times, we're going to look at these ABCs:

Acknowledge God's hand
Bloom where you are planted
Concentrate on God's promises
Do something useful
Expect to become a masterpiece

Interacting with God's Word

1. Who caused the Israelites to be carried away from Jerusalem to Babylon? (Jeremiah 29:4,7)?

   What command is given to the Israelites in Jeremiah 29:7?

2. What promises are given to the Jewish people in Jeremiah 29:10?

3. Read Jeremiah 29:14. Was there anything random about what had happened to God's people?

   Why?

4. What do we learn about God's sovereignty over the lives of people in the following passages?

   1 Samuel 2:6-8—

Psalm 75:7—

Psalm 135:6—

Proverbs 16:9—

Proverbs 19:21—

In what ways do the above passages apply to you?

Stepping Toward New Growth

This brings us to our first principle:

    Acknowledge God's hand

What difficult circumstance are you enduring now (or have you endured most recently)?

Have you acknowledged God's hand in it? How will doing this help you?

It's said that what you think about God will affect your perspective when problems come your way. What kinds of thoughts would a faulty and negative view of God produce?

What kinds of thoughts would a positive biblical view of God produce?

How would you describe your view of God in light of your current difficulties? What would you like to change?

Loving God with All Your Mind

No matter what happens in your life, you need to recognize God has allowed it. No matter how difficult or negative your situation, it is part of God's plan for you. When you accept this truth, you'll eliminate your fears, bewilderment, and anger. And you'll replace them with a trust that rests in God and a peace that knows God is watching over you.

What thoughts or habits can you cultivate that would help you to immediately acknowledge God's hand in every event in your life—no matter whether good or bad?

*D*ay 2—Bearing Fruit During Difficult Times

*W*hen life goes wrong, we have two choices: We can either complain and be miserable, or we can make the most of our situation.

After the Israelites were taken into captivity, God told them to go ahead and build homes, plant gardens, and grow families. He even urged them to pray for peace in Babylon. Instead of mourning their loss, the people were to settle down, take root, and bloom where God had planted them.

Too often we are guilty of waiting until life gets better. We say, "When life returns to normal, I'll get my act together." And we mope on the sidelines instead of making ourselves available for God's use. We remain barren in the hard times instead of bearing fruit.

Does that describe how you usually react to life's difficulties?

Interacting with God's Word

Our second principle for enduring through life's trials is...

Bloom where you are planted

1. In Acts 28:16, we read about Paul living under house arrest while in Rome. He was jailed for two years (verse 30). How did he use his time?

2. What do we learn from Philippians 1:12-13 about the way Paul used his time in Rome? According to verse 14, what additional benefit came from Paul's willingness to bloom where he was planted?

3. Genesis 39:1-6 tells what happened after Joseph was sold by his brothers and became a slave in Egypt. What evidence do you see that Joseph bloomed where he was planted?

4. Both Paul and Joseph faced severe hardships that few of us will ever face. But should we ever find ourselves in similar straits, what assurance are we given in Philippians 4:13?

   In light of the promise in Philippians 4:13, is there any place where it's impossible to bloom where we're planted?

5. Read Ephesians 5:15-17. What are we called to do (verse 15)?

   What are we to make the most of, and why (verse 16)?

   What are we to pursue (verse 17)?

Stepping Toward New Growth

Can you describe a situation or two in which you were uprooted and had to start over? Have you since bloomed where God planted you? How?

Think about an "assignment" God has given you that you haven't yet made the most of. What steps can you take toward blooming where you are planted?

How are you doing at blooming in the following areas of your life? And how can you do better at making the most of each circumstance?

Your relationship with God—

Your marriage and family relationships—

Your friendships—

Your church—

Your workplace—

Other—

Loving God with All Your Mind

Can you honestly say to God you are giving your all every day...no matter what your circumstances? By blooming where you are planted, what are you telling God?

"Wherever you are, be all there. Live to the hilt every situation you believe to be the will of God."

*—entry from Jim Elliot's journal
(Jim was a missionary martyred
in the jungles of Ecuador in 1956)*

*D*ay 3—Drawing Hope from God's Promises

⚬⚭⚬

*W*hen the people of Jerusalem were taken captive by the Babylonians, all looked hopeless. Their city was ruined, and the temple was destroyed. They lost their homes and belongings. They were taken to a strange land where people spoke a different language and worshipped pagan gods. They had to adapt to a new culture and obey the demands of their captors. Their world had been turned upside down, and their future looked grim.

But then God spoke a promise that would give them hope. He wanted them to know He had not abandoned or forgotten them. He said, "After seventy years are completed at Babylon, I will visit you and perform My good word toward you, and cause you to return to this place" (Jeremiah 29:10).

God's words of assurance gave His disillusioned people reason to have hope. His promise helped them to hang on and endure. And that's what God's promises can do for us as well. When the dark clouds of hardship block the sunlight, it doesn't mean the sun has disappeared. It's still there—we just can't see it. And God's promises are reminders to us that God is still with us, even when we cannot see Him.

Interacting with God's Word

This brings us to our third principle for enduring difficult times:

Concentrate on God's promises

1. What does the Bible say about the God who stands behind the promises of Scripture?

Psalm 89:8—

Psalm 119:90—

Lamentations 3:22-23—

1 Thessalonians 5:24—

2 Thessalonians 3:3—

Hebrews 10:23—

2. In light of God's faithfulness, how should we respond?

Psalm 92:1-2—

Psalm 119:147-148—

1 Peter 4:19—

Stepping Toward New Growth

What are some specific promises in Scripture that have brought hope and blessing to you in the past?

In what areas of your life do you need to place more confidence in God's promises?

What steps can you take to concentrate more on God's promises in the midst of dark times?

Loving God with All Your Mind

No matter how difficult your circumstance, you can have glorious hope even when all seems hopeless. Even when you feel as though God has forgotten you, you can have confidence He is very much present in your life. He knows what you are facing. He will give you strength to persevere. And He has plans for your life—plans that will come to fruition because no one can stop Him from fulfilling His purpose (Job 42:2).

When Paul asked God to remove the thorn in his flesh, God said no. Instead, he promised Paul a continual supply of grace that would help the apostle to endure his affliction. God said to Paul, "My grace is sufficient for you" (2 Corinthians 12:9).

God's grace is sufficient for you as well. In other words, there is no problem so great that it exceeds the grace God has given you to handle it. In every need you have, God's grace is more than sufficient. Write down the ways God has shown His sufficiency to you... then thank Him in prayer for what He has done.

$\mathcal{D}$ay 4—Becoming God's Masterpiece

$\mathcal{W}$hen we are discouraged, it's easy to become resigned from day-to-day life. When hard times come, our tendency is to give up and throw in the towel. We let discouragement and doubt paralyze us to the point of inaction.

But God wouldn't let that happen to His people when they were taken into captivity in Babylon. In Jeremiah 29, He told them to live as normally as they could in spite of their circumstances. He said to build homes, plant gardens, get married, and have families. No, this wasn't the time for them to "check out." They were to carry on and let God continue to work through them.

Earlier we studied God's promise in Romans 8:28 that "all things work together for good to those who love God." God can use *every* circumstance in life toward our ultimate good.

And there's another promise we can cling to when life gets rough: "Being confident of this very thing…He who has begun a good work in you will complete it until the day of Jesus Christ" (Philippians 1:6).

God is at work in you—through good times and bad—to make a beautiful masterpiece that will one day be complete. Nothing can prevent God from finishing His work in you!

Interacting with God's Word

This brings us to the final two guidelines in the ABCs of enduring difficult times:

Do something useful

Expect to become a masterpiece

First, let's look at what Scripture says about being useful.

1. Read 1 Corinthians 12:4-6. What do these verses say about the gifts, ministries, and activities done by believers?

For what purpose did God give spiritual gifts to each believer (verse 7)?

2. Read 1 Corinthians 12:15-22, then answer the following:

What point is made in verses 15-16?

What point is made in verse 17?

What does verse 19 go on to say?

What do verses 21-22 communicate?

3. Given what you've learned about the body of Christ in the above verses, what would you say to a Christian who feels "unneeded"?

4. Now read 2 Corinthians 1:3-4. In what way can God use even a hurting person?

5. And now for our last principle: Because it is the all-wise and all-powerful God who is at work in you, you can expect to become a masterpiece.

According to the following verses, what is God's ultimate purpose in your life?

Romans 8:29—

2 Corinthians 3:18—

Ephesians 4:13—

1 John 3:2—

Stepping Toward New Growth

Describe a couple of difficult situations in which you have felt useless to God. In each instance, what were some ways God did use you, or could have used you?

What are some ways you are presently useful in...

…your home?

…your church?

…your workplace?

…your school, or other significant place of interaction?

Where do you see room for new growth?

When it comes to enduring life's trials, how can the knowledge that you are becoming a masterpiece help you?

Loving God with All Your Mind

When it comes to your usefulness to God, don't listen to your feelings—especially when life gets rough! Trust the facts of Scripture. You have a unique place in the body of Christ. You are essential. You have something to offer to others, no matter how overwhelming your negative circumstances.

Can you think of other Christians who made themselves useful even when they faced great hardships? What can you learn from their example?

What evidence do you see in your life that you're a "masterpiece in progress"?

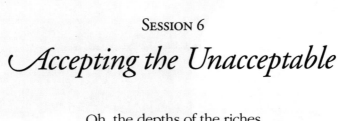

SESSION 6

Accepting the Unacceptable

Oh, the depths of the riches
both of the wisdom and knowledge of God!
How unsearchable are His judgments and
His ways past finding out!

ROMANS 11:33

*D*ay 1—When the Unexpected Happens

❦

*Y*ou can probably remember a day in your life when all of a sudden, the unexpected happened…and nothing was ever again the same. Maybe it was a phone call, a letter, an appointment at the doctor's office. And whatever it was that happened, you found yourself reeling from the impact. You were at a loss for words. You didn't know how to respond.

For Mary, the mother of Jesus, that moment came when the angel Gabriel announced she would conceive and bring forth a son. Surprised, Mary asked, "How can this be, since I do not know a man?" (Luke 1:34). Gabriel answered, "The Holy Spirit will come upon you, and the power of the Highest will overshadow you" (verse 35). In other words, this would be a miracle.

Though Mary could not understand how she became pregnant, she accepted God's plan for her life. She said, "Behold the maidservant of the Lord! Let it be to me according to your word" (verse 38).

Mary's life would never be the same. God spoke, and everything changed. People would long suspect Mary had committed adultery—what other explanation was possible for her pregnancy? Though this meant a cloud of doubt over Mary's reputation, she was willing to accept the "unacceptable." This humble maidservant said, in essence, "Whatever

God wants, I am willing to do." She had one purpose in her life: To obey her Master's will—quickly, quietly, and without question.

Interacting with God's Word

How can we respond as Mary did to the unexpected or difficult turning points in life? First, she recognized she wasn't her own—she belonged to God. That should be our perspective as well.

1. Read 1 Corinthians 6:19-20. What does verse 19 say about the Holy Spirit?

   Who does your body belong to (verse 19), and why (verse 20)?

   What command is given at the end of verse 20?

2. What does Romans 12:1-2 urge you to do?

3. What point does Paul make in Romans 14:7-8?

4. What is your supreme purpose, according to 1 Corinthians 10:31?

5. Based on the Bible verses you've just read, how are you to respond to God's desires for your life?

Stepping Toward New Growth

What are some of the key responsibilities God has placed in your life? Do you have the heart of a maidservant in fulfilling those responsibilities?

How have you reacted to unexpected and difficult turning points in the past? In what ways can you react better in the future?

How can learning to accept the unacceptable strengthen your relationship with God?

Loving God with All Your Mind

True love for God means having the heart of a willing servant. It means making yourself available for God's purposes. It means being ready to serve whenever He calls you, and wherever He calls you.

Are you willing to consent to God's will even when you can't comprehend it? Can you trust Him completely and accept the unacceptable? Can you say with Mary, "Behold the maidservant of the Lord! Let it be according to your word"?

Day 2—Accepting God's Wisdom and Knowledge

When it comes to accepting life's traumatic turning points, we have learned from Mary the wisdom of having a servant's heart. Because she saw herself as belonging to God, she was able to receive God's plan with grace and not bitterness.

Another reason Mary was so receptive is because she had a wonderful knowledge of God hidden in her heart. We see evidence of this in the song she sang to the Lord in Luke 1:46-55. In those 10 verses are at least 15 discernable references to the Old Testament—references that show she was familiar with God's character. She spoke of His might, holiness, mercy, strength, sovereignty, faithfulness, and more.

The better you know God, the more confidence and peace you'll experience in life's painful moments. When you know—and believe!—that God is too kind to do anything cruel and too wise to make a mistake, you'll find it easier to say, "God, I trust You. Though I don't understand, I know You'll take care of me."

Rather than ask *why* we are suffering, we need to look at *who* it is that's in control. What can we learn about the heavenly Father who watches over us? Romans 11:33 reveals four things we need to accept so we can more readily receive the unacceptable:

- God's wisdom
- God's knowledge

- God's judgments
- God's ways

Interacting with God's Word

Romans 11:33 begins, "Oh, the depth of the riches both of the wisdom and knowledge of God!" The Lord's wisdom and knowledge are infinitely beyond our understanding. He is the source of both.

1. What do you learn from the following verses about God's wisdom?

   Psalm 104:24—

   Psalm 147:5—

   Jeremiah 10:7—

   Daniel 2:20-21—

   James 1:5—

2. And about His knowledge?

   Job 37:16—

   Psalm 139:2—

Psalm 139:6—

Jeremiah 32:19—

Matthew 6:8—

3. God is the source of all there is to know, and He knows all that can be known. How can your awareness of these truths bring comfort to you in life's trials?

Stepping Toward New Growth

There is nothing that surprises God. His wisdom and knowledge are perfect and eternal. He knows how every circumstance will begin and end. With that in mind…

…how well do you think God understands the challenges you face?

…how well do you think God can help resolve your problems?

…how well do you think God can make "all things work together for good" (Romans 8:28)?

If you were to meet a believer who is having a hard time accepting the unacceptable, what would you tell her?

Loving God with All Your Mind

In the DVD session, I shared about the 6.8 Northridge earthquake that struck the part of Southern California where we lived. All four walls of books in our study had fallen to the floor—making the room a mass of chaos! To bring order out of the chaos, I looked for the bookends, then began placing the books, one by one, back on the shelves between the bookends.

When it comes to the chaos of life, you can do the same thing with the bookends of God's wisdom and knowledge. When things happen that you don't understand, you can "file them" between "the depth of the riches both of the wisdom and knowledge of God" (Romans 11:33).

What do you have in your life right now that you can surrender to your heavenly Father's wisdom and knowledge? Write them below, then take each one to Him in prayer… believing that He understands and He cares.

Day 3—Accepting God's Judgments

Are you able to trust God "in the dark"? Are you willing to trust Him even when you don't understand what is happening and why?

When God chose for Mary to give birth to Jesus, she didn't question His decision for her life. Rather, she simply said, "Let it be to me according to your word" (Luke 1:38). She submitted to His unsearchable judgment, which is beyond understanding.

In the sudden and unexpected turning points in life, frequently we have no idea what God is doing. As Romans 11:33 says, God's ways are "past finding out." The deep things of God are unknowable. Yet because of His perfect wisdom and knowledge, we can have confidence that His judgments—or decisions—are perfect as well.

Though it is not necessary for us to *figure out* God's judgments, it's vital that we *accept* them. For if we don't, we will find ourselves fighting against God. Whose judgment do you trust more—yours, or His?

Interacting with God's Word

1. Though we looked at Proverbs 3:5-6 earlier in this workbook, let's look at it again because it speaks to us about trusting God "in the dark."

According to verse 5, who are we to trust, and to what extent?

What should we not trust (verse 5)?

What command are we given in the first part of verse 6?

What will result when we obey that command (verse 6)?

How much of *you* do you see in those verses? How much of *God*?

How would you sum up Proverbs 3:5-6 in your own words?

After Job had suffered greatly, what remarkable statement did he make about God's judgments in Job 9:10?

What does Job's statement tell you about his view of God even after he lost all his children and possessions?

What verdict did Joseph give regarding God's judgments (decisions) after all the evil his brothers had done against him (Genesis 50:20)?

According to Psalm 19:11, what is the result of submitting to God's judgments?

For you to accept the unacceptable means placing complete trust in the judgments of God. It means submitting yourself to His plan without question.

Stepping Toward New Growth

In what areas of your life have you found yourself leaning on your own understanding?

What do you forfeit when you do that, according to Proverbs 3:6?

When you question God's judgments, what are you communicating to Him?

What would you rather communicate to Him instead?

Loving God with All Your Mind

How unsearchable are God's judgments! They are unfathomable, inexhaustible, inscrutable. And though we often cannot understand His decisions, we can trust them—completely!

Did you know it's not possible to doubt and trust God at the same time? The two are incompatible. The chart on the next page will help illustrate this point. In each of the categories, describe what *doubting God* and *trusting God* would look like in your life situations.

	Doubting God	Trusting God
My health		
My finances		
My job		
My relationships		
My spiritual growth		
My usefulness in church		
My daily needs		
My hurts and suffering		

What can you learn from this chart?

Based on what you see in the chart, what can you thank God for?

*D*ay 4—Accepting God's Ways

*B*ible teacher A.W. Tozer, in his classic book *The Knowledge of the Holy,* wrote,

> A right conception of God is basic not only to systematic theology but to practical Christian living as well...I believe there is scarcely an error in doctrine or a failure in applying Christian ethics that cannot be traced finally to imperfect and ignoble thoughts about God.*

Tozer was saying that incorrect thoughts about God will have a negative impact on your life. If you don't know and truly believe what the Bible says about God's wisdom, justice, power, sovereignty, holiness, goodness, lovingkindness, mercy, compassion, and grace, it's going to have a negative effect on your everyday life.

That's why it's so important for us to get to know God! That's what we're doing right now as we continue studying Romans 11:33, which proclaims the infinitely great wisdom, knowledge, judgments, and ways of God.

We've already looked at what Scripture says about God's wisdom, knowledge, and judgments. Let's learn now about His ways, which are "past finding out!"

---

* A.W. Tozer, *The Knowledge of the Holy* (New York: Harper & Row, 1961), p. 10.

Interacting with God's Word

1. What does God say about His ways in Isaiah 55:8?

How does God illustrate this in verse 9?

What does this tell you about God's ways as compared to yours?

2. What do you learn from Isaiah 40:13?

3. How are God's works described in Job 9:10?

4. Read Job 36:22-23. What do those verses tell you about God? About man?

Stepping Toward New Growth

Can you think of a time when you thought God would do one thing, only to see Him do something completely different or unexpected? What were you expecting? How did God answer? What did you learn?

Is there a "roadblock" that is holding you back in life? That is, a situation beyond your control that you wish you could change? Maybe it has to do with your marriage, your family, your job, or your ministry service at church. Have you considered that perhaps God is allowing that situation to hold you back? Why might God do that?

How well are you doing at accepting the unacceptable? Do you find yourself resisting God at certain points? What do you need to let go of and turn over to Him? What does it really mean to let God be God?

Loving God with All Your Mind

The apostle Paul wrote Romans 11:33 as a doxology of praise to God. In the chapters previous to Romans 11, Paul had written of God's many mighty works on our behalf. And by the time he gets to Romans 11:33, he can no longer hold himself back. He breaks forth into praise, declaring the infinite greatness and majesty of God.

What are some examples of God's unsearchable wisdom, knowledge, judgments, and ways that you have seen in your life? Write down four or five of them here...then take time to break forth in praise and thank Him for what He has done!

A Final Word:
Growing in Your Love for God

What a privilege it has been to share with you my six most life-changing memory verses! My prayer is that you're already experiencing their life-changing power, and that they have given you a deeper appreciation for all God does for us.

If you haven't already started committing these verses to memory, I strongly encourage you to do so. You'll find them a source of wisdom, comfort, and direction in virtually every area of your life. No matter what comes your way—even the most devastating of circumstances—these verses hold the answers that can help you hang on, endure, and keep your focus upon God.

So that you can benefit from these verses one more time in this study, I've listed them below for you. Read each verse, then answer the questions that follow. My hope for you is that you'll let these verses continue to transform your life!

> *Finally, brethren, whatever things are true, whatever things are noble, whatever things are just, whatever things are pure, whatever things are lovely, whatever things are of good report, if there is any virtue and if there is anything praiseworthy—meditate on these things* (Philippians 4:8).

What stands out to you the most about this verse?

How has this verse helped elevate your view of God?

How does this verse help you to love God with all your mind?

Do not worry about tomorrow, for tomorrow will worry about its own things. Sufficient for the day is its own trouble (Matthew 6:34).

What stands out to you the most about this verse?

How has this verse helped elevate your view of God?

How does this verse help you to love God with all your mind?

Brethren, I do not count myself to have apprehended; but one thing I do, forgetting those things which are behind and reaching for those things which are ahead, I press toward the goal for the prize of the upward call of God in Christ Jesus (Philippians 3:13-14).

What stands out to you the most about this verse?

How has this verse helped elevate your view of God?

How does this verse help you to love God with all your mind?

> *We know that all things work together for good to those who love God, to those who are called according to His purpose* (Romans 8:28).

What stands out to you the most about this verse?

How has this verse helped elevate your view of God?

How does this verse help you to love God with all your mind?

> *For I know the thoughts I think toward you, says the LORD, thoughts of peace and not of evil, to give you a future and a hope* (Jeremiah 29:11).

What stands out to you the most about this verse?

How has this verse helped elevate your view of God?

How does this verse help you to love God with all your mind?

Oh, the depths of the riches both of the wisdom and knowledge of God! How unsearchable are His judgments and His ways past finding out! (Romans 11:33).

What stands out to you the most about this verse?

How has this verse helped elevate your view of God?

How does this verse help you to love God with all your mind?

Loving God with All Your Mind

If you've benefited from the *Loving God with All Your Mind* DVD series and interactive workbook, you'll want to get Elizabeth George's bestselling book *Loving God with All Your Mind*.

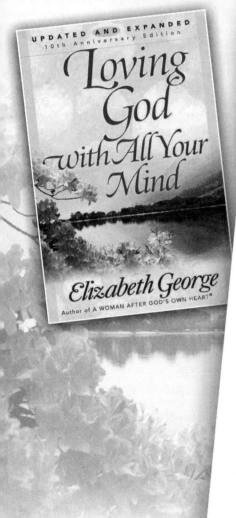

Dear friend,

It's been such a joy for me to share a little of my life and a lot about God's Word with you through this study. I've been picturing and imagining you and your life, and praying all the way through that these powerful—and probably familiar verses will strengthen and encourage you.

However, I cannot encourage you enough to read my book *Loving God with All Your Mind*. It was born out of my personal struggles, and the application of these six verses has stimulated great spiritual growth in my walk with God, all to His praise and honor and glory. What you've gained from this study will be enhanced and become more fixed in your heart and mind. You'll become aware of how these amazing verses can be applied to the many facets of your daily life and to any future challenges you encounter.

Best of all, we can continue our friendship as we seek together to love our Lord even more.

In His everlasting love,

Elizabeth George

Books by Elizabeth George

- Beautiful in God's Eyes
- Beautiful in God's Eyes for Young Women
- Breaking the Worry Habit...Forever
- Finding God's Path Through Your Trials
- Following God with All Your Heart
- The Heart of a Woman Who Prays
- Life Management for Busy Women
- Loving God with All Your Mind
- Loving God with All Your Mind DVD and Workbook
- A Mom After God's Own Heart
- A Mom After God's Own Heart Devotional
- Moments of Grace for a Woman's Heart
- One-Minute Inspiration for Women
- Prayers to Calm Your Heart
- Quiet Confidence for a Woman's Heart
- Raising a Daughter After God's Own Heart
- The Remarkable Women of the Bible
- Small Changes for a Better Life
- Walking with the Women of the Bible
- A Wife After God's Own Heart
- A Woman After God's Own Heart®
- A Woman After God's Own Heart®— Daily Devotional
- A Woman's Daily Walk with God
- A Woman's Guide to Making Right Choices
- A Woman's High Calling
- A Woman's Walk with God
- A Woman Who Reflects the Heart of Jesus
- A Young Woman After God's Own Heart
- A Young Woman After God's Own Heart— A Devotional
- A Young Woman's Guide to Discovering Her Bible
- A Young Woman's Guide to Making Right Choices
- A Young Woman's Guide to Prayer
- A Young Woman Who Reflects the Heart of Jesus

Study Guides

- Beautiful in God's Eyes Growth & Study Guide
- Finding God's Path Through Your Trials Growth & Study Guide
- Following God with All Your Heart Growth & Study Guide
- Life Management for Busy Women Growth & Study Guide
- Loving God with All Your Mind Growth & Study Guide
- Loving God with All Your Mind Interactive Workbook
- A Mom After God's Own Heart Growth & Study Guide
- The Remarkable Women of the Bible Growth & Study Guide
- Small Changes for a Better Life Growth & Study Guide
- A Wife After God's Own Heart Growth & Study Guide
- A Woman After God's Own Heart® Growth & Study Guide
- A Woman's Call to Prayer Growth & Study Guide
- A Woman's High Calling Growth & Study Guide
- A Woman Who Reflects the Heart of Jesus Growth & Study Guide

Children's Books

- A Girl After God's Own Heart
- A Girl After God's Own Heart Devotional
- A Girl's Guide to Making Really Good Choices
- God's Wisdom for Little Girls
- A Little Girl After God's Own Heart

Books by Jim George

- 10 Minutes to Knowing the Men and Women of the Bible
- The Bare Bones Bible® Handbook
- The Bare Bones Bible® Handbook for Teens
- A Boy After God's Own Heart
- A Boy's Guide to Making Really Good Choices
- A Dad After God's Own Heart
- A Husband After God's Own Heart
- Know Your Bible from A to Z
- A Leader After God's Own Heart
- A Man After God's Own Heart
- A Man After God's Own Heart Devotional
- The Man Who Makes a Difference
- One-Minute Insights for Men
- A Young Man After God's Own Heart
- A Young Man's Guide to Discovering His Bible
- A Young Man's Guide to Making Right Choices

Books by Jim & Elizabeth George

- A Couple After God's Own Heart
- A Couple After God's Own Heart Interactive Workbook
- God's Wisdom for Little Boys
- A Little Boy After God's Own Heart